Our Global Community

Homes

Cassie Mayer

Heinemann Library
Chicago, Illinois

© 2007 Heinemann Library
a division of Reed Elsevier Inc.
Chicago, Illinois

Customer Service 888-454-2279
Visit our website at www.heinemannraintree.com

Designed by Joanna Hinton-Malivoire
Photo research by Ruth Smith
Printed and bound in China by South China Printing Co. Ltd.

11 10 09 08
10 9 8 7 6 5 4 3 2

The Library of Congress has cataloged the first edition of this book as follows:
Mayer, Cassie.
  Homes / Cassie Mayer.
    p. cm. -- (Our global community)
  Includes bibliographical references and index.
  ISBN 978-1-4034-9399-6 (hc) -- ISBN 978-1-4034-9408-5 (pb) 1. Dwellings--Juvenile literature. I. Title.
  GT172.M39 2007
  392.3'6--dc22

                                        2006034294

Acknowledgements
The publishers would like to thank the following for permission to reproduce photographs: Alamy Images pp. **9** (blickwinkel), **13** (DY Riess MD), **15** (photoz.at), **16** (Neil McAllister), **17** (Anders Ryman), **20** (Petr Svarc), **23** (photoz.at); Corbis pp. **6** (Jan Butchofsky-Houser), **10** (Bo Zaunders), **11** (J. Scott Smith/Beateworks), **14** (Jan Butchofsky-Houser), **18** (Jacques Langevin), **19** (Michael S. Yamashita), **21**, **23** (Jacques Langevin); Getty Images pp. **4** (Iconica), **5** (Image Bank), **7** (Stone), **8** (Iconica), **23** (Iconica); Lonely Planet Images p. **12** (Ariadne Van Zandbergen).

Cover photograph reproduced with permission of Getty Images/Imagebank. Back cover photograph reproduced with permission of Lonely Planet Images/Ariadne Van Zandbergen.

Every effort has been made to contact copyright holders of any material reproduced in this book. Any omissions will be rectified in subsequent printings if notice is given to the publishers.

The paper used to print this books comes from sustainable resources.

Contents

Homes Around the World

People live in homes.

Homes are big and small.
Homes are tall and short.

Types of Homes

Homes are close together.

Homes are far apart.

Homes are in hot places.

Homes are in cold places.

Homes are old.

Homes are new.

Homes are made of mud.

Homes are made of stone.

Homes are made of sticks.

stilt

Homes rest on stilts.

Special Homes

Homes float on water.

Homes sit in trees.

Some homes can be moved.

Most homes stay in one place.

Homes are different around the world.

All homes give shelter.

What Are Homes Made of?

- Wood comes from trees.

- Stones come from the ground.

- Mud comes from the earth.

- Bricks are made of clay. Clay is mud. It is heated to make hard bricks.

- Concrete is made of gravel, sand, and water.

Picture Glossary

home the place where you live

shelter safety

stilt pole that a home rests on. Stilts keep homes above water.

Index

Note to Parents and Teachers
This series expands children's horizons beyond their neighborhoods to show that communities around the world share similar features and rituals of daily life. The text has been chosen with the advice of a literacy expert to ensure that beginners can read the books independently or with moderate support. Stunning photographs visually support the text while engaging students with the material.

You can support children's nonfiction literacy skills by helping students use the table of contents, headings, picture glossary, and index.